What is the relationship between awareness, perception and experience?

John King

123 Books

Copyright © 2011 by John King

All rights reserved. This book, or parts thereof, may not be reproduced in any form without permission.

A catalogue record for this book is available from the British Library

ISBN: 978-1-907962-33-2

Published by 123 Books

Reading, England

For Becky

Contents

Introduction   7

What is the relationship between awareness, perception and experience?   9

Introduction

There are a very diverse range of views concerning the nature of awareness, perception and experience. This diversity of views applies both to the nature of each of the individual phenomena considered in isolation, and to the links between the different phenomena.

Another issue where there are a very diverse range of views is the question of how pervasive the various phenomena are in the universe. For instance: Do atoms perceive? Do atoms experience? Are atoms aware?

Awareness, perception & experience

The prime aim of the essay contained in this book is to explore the nature of the individual phenomena and the possible nature of the relationships between the phenomena, rather than to focus on the issue of the pervasiveness of the phenomena in the universe. Although, it should be noted, the nature of the phenomena and the relationships between the three phenomena will be of importance to the issue of pervasiveness. This is because certain relationships entail that greater pervasiveness is more plausible, whilst other relationships entail that less pervasiveness is more plausible.

What is the relationship between awareness, perception and experience?

There are numerous possible relationships between the phenomena of awareness, experience and perception. In this book my aim is to consider these various possible relationships with the purpose of attempting to make some progress in understanding how these three phenomena are actually related.

This attempt is not aided by the fact that I can only know about what I am aware of (and you can only know about what you aware of). By this I am simply stating an obvious fact about one's relationship with the world. So, one cannot know if there are states of feeling, or states of awareness, in that which is not one – for example, in a stone or in a bumble bee. Similarly, one cannot know anything about the Eiffel Tower if one has never become aware of the existence of the Eiffel Tower (one has never visited it, seen pictures of it, heard anyone talk about it, etc).

One is ignorant about the states of the world that one is not aware of. However, it would obviously be woefully inadequate to simply assert that what one is not aware of does not exist. The simple fact that one *cannot become aware* of the states within bumble bees and stones does not mean that these states do not exist; just as one's *lack of awareness of the existence of* the Eiffel Tower does not mean that the Eiffel Tower does not exist. There is clearly an important difference between that which one is not aware of but could become aware of, and that which one is not aware of and cannot become aware of.

Let us consider those states of the world that one is not aware of and cannot become aware of. How should one think of these states? Well, I take it to be obvious that one should accept that one does not know the nature of the states that one is not aware of. This means that one should accept the possibility of 'perception without awareness' and 'experience without awareness'.

Awareness, perception & experience

In the first part of the essay I consider the possibility that experience and awareness are equivalent – I call this position the 'awareness as experience' paradigm. In the next part of the essay I consider the possibility that experience can exist without awareness. Then, in order to complete the analysis of the relationship between experience and awareness, I consider the possibility that awareness can exist without experience.

I then turn to the possible relationships that could exist between perception and awareness. Having done this I then consider the possible relationships that could exist between perception and experience. A full understanding of the relationship between the three phenomena clearly requires an appreciation of how they relate to sleep and dreaming; so, I also consider this topic. Finally, I draw some conclusions.

Awareness as experience

A widespread contemporary view of the relationship between awareness and experience is that the two phenomena are the same thing; on this view 'awareness' and 'experience' are words that refer to the same state of the world. According to this view there is no such thing as a state of experience which is wholly devoid of awareness, and there is no such thing as a state of awareness which is wholly devoid of experience. In other words, according to this view

Awareness, perception & experience

a *single state* of the world exists which is intrinsically and necessarily both experience-involving and awareness-involving. Various terms are used by the advocates of this view to refer to the *experience-involving* part of this state – 'experience', 'something it is like', 'qualia', 'feeling', 'what-it's likeness', and 'qualitative feeling' (I will often use the term 'what-it-is-likeness' to refer to the *experience-involving* part of this state). When it comes to the *awareness-involving* part of this state it is typically referred to by the words 'awareness', 'conscious' and 'consciousness'. Here are some assertions by advocates of the dominant 'awareness as experience' paradigm:

The most remarkable fact about the universe is that certain parts of it are conscious. Somehow nature has managed to pull the rabbit of experience out of a hat made of mere matter. (William Seager)[1]

We can say that a being is conscious if there is *something it is like* to be that being.
(David Chalmers)[2]

---

[1] William Seager, *Theories of Consciousness*, Routledge, London, 1999, p. i.

[2] David Chalmers, *The Conscious Mind*, OUP, Oxford, 1996, p. 4.

Awareness, perception & experience

> I use the word "consciousness" to mean, roughly, experience. And I think of experience, broadly, as encompassing thinking, feeling, and the fact that a world "shows up" for us in perception. (Alva Noe)[3]

> experience always involves some minimal awareness (David Griffin)[4]

---

[3] Alva Noe, *Out of Our Heads*, Hill and Wong, New York, 2009, p. 8.

[4] David Griffin, *Unsnarling the World-Knot*, London: University of California Press, 1998, p. 131.

Consciousness, as I understand it, is the property things have when there is *something that it is like to be them*. (Philip Goff)[5]

Consciousness...is part of our oldest biological endowment. Remember that we are dealing with the phenomenon of sentience, of feeling, seeing, smelling, and so on.

(Colin McGinn)[6]

---

[5] Philip Goff, *Should Materialists be afraid of Ghosts*, PhD Thesis, University of Reading, 2006, p. 1.

[6] Colin McGinn, *The Mysterious Flame*, Basic Books, USA, 1999, pp. 62-3.

Awareness, perception & experience

> It is a remarkable fact about consciousness...that there is a qualitative feel to any conscious state. (John Searle)[7]

experience, 'consciousness', conscious experience, 'phenomenology', experiential 'what-it's likeness', feeling, sensation, explicit conscious thought as we have it and know it at almost every waking moment. Many words are used to denote this necessarily occurrent (essentially non-dispositional) phenomenon, and I will use the terms 'experience', 'experi-

---

[7] John Searle, *Conversations on Consciousness*, OUP, Oxford, 2005, p. 202.

ential phenomena' and 'experientiality' to refer to it. (Galen Strawson)[8]

These quotes indicate the contemporary pervasiveness of this view; this view is very widely held and it encompasses people who espouse very diverse views. Of those quoted above we have the 'naturalistic dualism' of Chalmers, the 'mysterianism' of McGinn, the 'biological naturalism' of Searle, the 'substance dualism' of Goff, and the 'panpsychism' of Strawson. Despite their diverse views all of these people are united by their belief in 'awareness as

---

[8] Galen Strawson, *Consciousness and its place in nature*, Imprint Academic, Exeter, 2006, p. 3.

experience'. This view can be seen as entailing the following two claims:

> *Awareness is an experience-involving state of the world.*

> *Experience is an awareness-involving state of the world.*

It is the second of these claims which is the most dubious – it is a claim that many people reject. If the second claim can be refuted through showing that experience can exist without awareness, then clearly this dominant paradigm is false. So, let us turn to the possibility of experience without awareness.

Experience without Awareness

Are there good reasons to believe that experience/'what-it-is-likeness' – can exist in the absence of awareness? There are two philosophical paradigms which entail the existence of experience without awareness. The first of these is the 'higher-order monitoring' theory of awareness – advocates of this position believe that states of experience can exist in one without awareness. The second paradigm is 'panexperientialism' – this is the view, as I

Awareness, perception & experience

am using the term here, that *all* states of the world are experiential but only a small minority of states of the world have awareness. Let us look at these two paradigms in turn.

Higher-Order Monitoring

In the western philosophical tradition the roots of the 'higher-order monitoring' view of awareness are usually traced back to the 'inner sense' view of John Locke. Locke asserted that: "the perception of the operations of our own mind within us...might properly enough be called internal sense."[9] In accordance with this assertion Locke defined awareness as follows: "Consciousness is the perception of what passes in a man's own mind"[10].

In contemporary philosophy there are two groups of 'higher-order monitoring' theorists. Both of these groups share the belief that awareness is an inner sense that exists at a 'higher order' and is directed towards lower level mental states; their disagreement is over whether the 'higher-order' is

---

[9] John Locke, *An Essay Concerning Human Understanding*, Oxford University Press, London, Volume 1, Book 2, Chapter 1, Section 4, p. 123.

[10] John Locke, *An Essay Concerning Human Understanding*, Oxford University Press, London, Volume 1, Book 2, Chapter 1, Section 19, p. 138.

perception-like or thought-like. David Armstrong and William Lycan advocate Higher-Order Perception (HOP) theories, whilst David Rosenthal advocates a Higher-Order Thought (HOT) theory. Let us look briefly at these theories with our main concern being their arguments that experience can exist without awareness.

Lycan argues that: "consciousness is the functioning of internal *attention mechanisms* directed at lower-order psychological states and events"[11]. When it comes to the link between awareness and experience Lycan claims that:

---

[11] William Lycan, *Consciousness and Experience*, MIT Press, London, 1996, p. 14.

the inner-sense theorist hardly need hold that monitoring does bring qualia into being. The monitoring only makes the subject aware of a quale that was there, independently, in the first place...the inner-sense theory is simply not a theory of what makes a state qualitative in the first place.[12]

Armstrong claims that: "Consciousness is a self-scanning mechanism in the central nervous system."[13] When it comes to the link between awareness and experience Armstrong argues that

---

[12] William Lycan, *Consciousness and Experience*, MIT Press, London, 1996, p. 43

[13] David Armstrong, *Nature of Mind and Other Essays*, University of Queensland Press, St Lucia, 1980, p. 15.

Awareness, perception & experience

sensations can exist without awareness (he calls this *minimal consciousness*); he also argues that perceptions of one's "environment and bodily state"[14] can exist without awareness (he calls this *perceptual consciousness*). According to Armstrong, awareness (which he calls *introspective consciousness*) is distinct from these experiential events: "Without introspective consciousness, we would not be aware that we existed"[15].

In contrast, David Rosenthal claims that the higher-order is not perception-like but that is

---

[14] David Armstrong, *Nature of Mind and Other Essays*, University of Queensland Press, St Lucia, 1980, p. 59.

[15] David Armstrong, *Nature of Mind and Other Essays*, University of Queensland Press, St Lucia, 1980, p. 67.

constituted by thought: "We are conscious of something, on this model, when we have a thought about it."[16] When it comes to the link between awareness and experience Rosenthal claims that:

> If we are intermittently unaware of a pain by being distracted from it, we feel the pain only intermittently; similarly with its hurting and our being in pain. Still, it is natural to speak of having had a pain that lasted throughout the day, and even to say that one was not always aware of that pain. This provides evidence that commonsense countenances

---

[16] David Rosenthal, "A Theory of Consciousness", in *The Nature of Consciousness*, Ed. N. Block, O. Flanagan, G. Guzeldere, MIT Press, London, 1997, p. 741.

the existence of nonconscious pains. Feeling pains and having them seem equivalent only because of our lack of interest in the nonconscious cases.[17]

So, the 'higher-order monitoring' theorists believe that experiences — such as the 'what-it-is-likeness' of a pain — can exist without awareness. It is worth mentioning that if the monitoring were to be reconceptualised as a 'same-order' phenomenon then the arguments for the disparity between experience and awareness would still apply.

---

[17] David Rosenthal, "A Theory of Consciousness", in *The Nature of Consciousness*, Ed. N. Block, O. Flanagan, G. Guzeldere, MIT Press, London, 1997, p. 732.

John King

Panexperientialism

I am using the term panexperientialism to refer to the view that every state of the world is experience-involving, but that only a very few states of the world are awareness-involving. Advocates of this view assert that it is unintelligible to suppose that the experiential could emerge out of the wholly unexperiential through a process of gradual evolution. However, they believe that the emergence of the aware out of the unaware is intelligible. Along these lines Gregg Rosenberg states that:

Panexperientialism is the view that experience exists throughout nature and that mentality (i.e., a thing requiring cognition, functionally construed) is not essential to it.[18]

the pretheoretical probability is that cognition merely represents a specific context wherein a more ubiquitous natural basis for experience expresses itself...our fundamental laws are likely to have panexperientialist consequences.[19]

---

[18] Gregg Rosenberg, *A Place for Consciousness*, Oxford University Press, Oxford, 2004, p. 91.

[19] Gregg Rosenberg, *A Place for Consciousness*, Oxford University Press, Oxford, 2004, p. 113.

If one is a panexperientialist then one will believe that the overwhelming majority of states in the world are experience-involving *but not* awareness-involving.

The existence of experience without awareness

We have considered two different reasons why one might assert that experience can exist without awareness. Either one can believe that awareness is a type of higher-order monitoring, or one can believe that the world is pervaded by experience but not awareness. Of course, it is also possible that one believes *both* that the world is pervaded by experience *and* that awareness is a type of higher-order monitoring. These two paradigms – 'panexperientialism' and 'higher-order monitoring' – have numerous supporters so the possibility of experience without awareness has to be acknowledged as a serious possibility.

Awareness without Experience

The question before us is whether a state of awareness is necessarily experience-involving. Awareness is awareness of something, and experience is a state of 'what-it-is-likeness'. If awareness is aware of an experience then it is clearly experience-involving. Is it necessarily the case that the 'something' that awareness is awareness of is an experiential something? If so, then awareness is necessarily experience-involving. Furthermore, is it possible that awareness can take itself as its own 'something'? If so, then part of the issue of whether awareness is necessarily experience-involving is the question of whether awareness is itself an intrinsically experiential entity. If awareness is an intrinsically experiential entity then when awareness takes any 'something' as an object this taking would be an experiential event – this would be the case even if the 'something' is itself a wholly unexperiential something and it would also be the case were awareness to take itself as a 'something'.

What kind of things (apart from itself) could awareness possibly become aware of? Well, the possible 'somethings' which can be the object of a state of awareness are states of experience, the perceptions of the senses, and thoughts. If the 'something' is a 'bodily feeling' then the state of awareness is experience-involving. If the 'something' is a perception by one of the senses then the state of awareness will be experience-involving. However, if 'thought' is wholly devoid of 'what-it-is-likeness' (let us assume that this is so) and the 'something' is a thought, then the state of awareness will not be experience-involving unless awareness is itself an intrinsically experiential entity.

So, is awareness an intrinsically experiential entity? This seems to be a difficult question to answer. If one accepts that panexperientialism is true then it seems that awareness would be an intrinsically experiential entity. This is because awareness is a state of the world and according to panexperientialism the entire world is pervaded by experiential states. However, things are not as simple as this. One can be a panexperientialist and still consistently hold that some phenomena which are located in the world are not experiential. For example, one could hold that the states of my brain that are responsible for generating a thought are themselves experiential states, but that the thought state that is generated by a particular arrangement of these experiential states is not *itself* an experiential state. In this scenario thought is a wholly non-experiential state of the world which supervenes on experiential states of the world. This supervenience relationship means that one could not isolate a particular part of the world and assert that "this state of the world is wholly nonexperiential"; however, it still follows that thought would be a state of the world that is wholly nonexperiential. Could a similar account be given for the phenomena of awareness? It could, so even if one is a panexperientialist one could still hold that awareness is not an intrinsically experiential entity.

Of course, one could reject panexperientialism. However, due to our conclusions from the previous paragraph this rejection will not be of any import to our current concern – one could still either assert that awareness is an intrinsically experiential entity or that it is an intrinsically unexperiential entity. If one asserts the latter and also accepts *either* that there are unexperiential 'somethings' such as thought *or* that awareness is able to take itself as its own 'something', then one will conclude that there can be awareness without experience.

So, if awareness is an intrinsically experiential entity, then there cannot be awareness without experience. However, it is quite possible that awareness is not an intrinsically experiential entity. If this is so, then when awareness takes a thought as a 'something' there will be awareness without experience; furthermore, if awareness can take itself as its own something, then this will also be an instance of awareness without experience.

Awareness, perception & experience

Perception and awareness

What is the relationship between perception and awareness? This is a complex question. I believe that there are two different types of perception. The first type arises from the operation of the senses (there is a serious debate – which I won't go into here – concerning how many human senses there are. For more on this, see my book: "Two Essays – What is 'What-it-is-likeness'? & How many human senses are there?").

The second type is the 'feeling perceptions' which are located throughout my body. By this I mean that when one becomes aware of a feeling state in one's leg (such as pain) this feeling state entails the part of the leg that is in pain perceiving the part of the world which caused it to become a 'painful' state. On this view, any movement in my body results in contact and this contact entails the interacting entities perceiving each other; this perception is simultaneously a feeling.

Despite the existence of two different types of perception a general definition of perception can be given:

> *Perception is a state of the world that obtains information about another state of the world*

Awareness, perception & experience

Now, the issue before us is the link between perception and awareness. There are obviously close links between perception and awareness. After all, 'perception' is the obtaining of information about another state of the world – so, it has a 'something' other than itself as its object. Similarly, 'awareness' is also a state of the world that takes a 'something' as its object. One could perhaps be forgiven for conflating perception and awareness and believing that they were one and the same state of the world. However, this would surely be a grave error. For, it is surely the case that awareness itself takes states of perception as its 'something'. That is, strictly speaking, one should never say that one becomes aware of a 'raindrop'; one should say that one becomes aware of one's perception of a raindrop (saying that one becomes "aware of a raindrop" is a useful shorthand, but it doesn't accurately reflect the processes which are going on in the world).

Is the relationship between perception and awareness that is outlined in the previous paragraph a widely accepted one? Seemingly not, as perception is typically defined in terms of awareness. A standard definition of the word perceive is:

> To apprehend through one of the senses, esp. sight; to become aware of by seeing, hearing, etc.; to see; to detect."[20]

---

[20] Oxford English Dictionary, http://dictionary.oed.com/cgi/entry/50175079?single=1&qu

Awareness, perception & experience

Clearly this definition implies that there is a singular state of the world which is both perception-involving and awareness-involving. On this view:

Perception is an awareness-involving state of the world

In other words, on this view perception cannot exist without awareness. Is this an acceptable view? If awareness takes 'perceptions' as its 'something' then it is obviously the case that perceptions can exist without being so taken; that is to say, percep-

---

ery_type=word&queryword=perceive&first=1&max_to_show=10 [accessed 8 February 2009]

tions could exist without awareness. Are there good reasons to accept that perceptions can exist without awareness? It is to this issue that we now turn.

Perception without awareness

Are there perceptions within one that are unaccompanied by awareness? The purpose of this section is to suggest that the answer to this question is yes. Let us consider some of the recent evidence from neuroscience and neuropsychology which supports this belief:

> Twenty (or even ten) years ago a researcher arguing for the existence of subliminal effects

was on the fringe of the discipline, on the outside looking in. Now a researcher arguing against the existence of subliminal effects is in that position, while the advocate sits squarely within the mainstream.[21]

[A development] that is unique to this age, is the virtual epidemic of dissociations discovered by neuropsychologists whereby residual processing occurs in the absence of acknowledged awareness...blindsight, blind-touch, 'deaf hearing', prosopagnosia and other

---

[21] Robert F. Bornstein, "Perception Without Awareness: Retrospect and Prospect", in Ed. Robert F. Bornstein, Thane S. Pittman, *Perception Without Awareness*, Guilford Press, London, 1992, p. 4.

forms of agnosia, dyslexia, unilateral neglect, and aphasia.[22]

while some physiological processes which result from sensory stimulation with light or sound may give rise to awareness of the stimulus, such phenomenal representation is neither a necessary consequence of effective stimulation, nor a necessary prelude to an overt response.[23]

---

[22] Lawrence Weiskrantz, "Introduction: Dissociated Issues", in Ed. A. D. Milner, M. D. Rugg, *The Neuropsychology of Consciousness*, Academic Press Ltd., London, 1992, p. 2.

[23] N. F. Dixon, *Subliminal Perception - The Nature of a Controversy*, McGraw-Hill, London, 1971, p. 2.

Awareness, perception & experience

How is one to conceptualise the relationship between perception and awareness given this evidence for perception without awareness? The best way is surely to think of things that perceive the world as engaged in a process of *continuous* perception of the world; whether these perceptions enter awareness is an entirely separate issue. In other words, even when one is wholly devoid of awareness one's senses will still perceive the world. In support of this view neuroscientist Rodolfo Llinas claims that:

> If, while you are awake, someone whispers to you that there is a bee in your hair, you will most likely do something about it. If, on the other hand, you are asleep when they whis-

per, you most likely won't. If this same scenario of comparisons were under experimental conditions where it was possible to monitor the flow of auditory information from your ear into your brain, we would see that this sensory signal is transduced peripherally, **in full regalia**, in both circumstances (waking and sleep). Why don't you hear it when asleep? ...The internal context of the brain during sleep is one that does not grant significance to the meaning of those whispered words or much of any auditory information save for the very loud.[24]

---

[24] Rodolfo Llinas, *i of the vortex – From Neurons to Self*, MIT Press, Massachusetts, 2002, p. 118.

The fact that the auditory apparatus processes the information "in full regalia" obviously implies that the sound was perceived. The reason for the lack of response when asleep is surely simply because there is no awareness of this perception. In other words, the "internal context of the brain during sleep" is one in which there is no awareness of the perceptions of one's auditory apparatus. There are perceptions without awareness. Of course, if there is a very loud sound perceived then this will cause one to stop sleeping/regain awareness.

Much of the recent scientific evidence for perception without awareness has come from investigating brain damage. Lawrence Weiskrantz asserts that: "in virtually all of the major cognitive categories that are disturbed by brain damage, there can be remarkably preserved functioning without the patients themselves being aware of this"[25]. One of the most well known examples of such dissociation is the phenomenon of 'blindsight' which occurs when visual stimuli can be discriminated without being seen. Humans with 'blindsight' claim that they are not aware of objects which are immediately in front of them. However, when they are persuaded to guess about whether the objects are moving in a certain direction they are able to do so the vast majority of the time. When these people are informed that they have actually perceived the

---

[25] Lawrence Weiskrantz, *Consciousness Lost and Found*, OUP, New York, 1999, p. 8.

correct movements of the objects in the vast majority of cases, they are greatly surprised. The phenomenon of 'blindsight' reveals that it is possible for humans to detect and localise visual stimuli without awareness that they are doing so.

Melvyn Goodale and David Milner have recently provided an account of the visual system which explains both blindsight and other cases of visual perception without awareness. They argue that there are two visual perceptual systems – the 'dorsal action system' which can never enter awareness, and the 'ventral perceptual system' which can potentially enter awareness. They assert that:

Rather than evolving some kind of general-purpose visual system that does everything, the brain has opted for two quite separate visual systems: one that guides our actions and another, quite separate system, that handles our perception.[26]

the visuomotor networks [of the dorsal action stream] no more need conscious representations of the world than does an industrial robot. The primary role of perceptual representations [of the ventral perceptual system] is not in the *execution* of actions but rather in helping the

---

[26] Melvyn Goodale, David Milner, *Sight Unseen*, OUP, Oxford, 2004, p. 30.

Awareness, perception & experience

person or animal to arrive at a decision to act in a particular way.[27]

After presenting a plethora of scientific evidence to support their view they conclude that: "there remains a whole realm of visual processing that we can never experience or reflect on. We are certainly aware of the actions that these visuomotor systems control, but we have no direct experience of the visual information they use."[28]

So, this is further clear support for the existence of perception without awareness. On this account

---

[27] Melvyn Goodale, David Milner, *Sight Unseen*, OUP, Oxford, 2004, pp. 47-48.

[28] Melvyn Goodale, David Milner, *Sight Unseen*, OUP, Oxford, 2004, p. 55.

information is obtained from the world and is used to control action, but it can never enter awareness. Goodale and Milner themselves deny that the activity of the *dorsal action stream* entails 'perception', this is because they use an inadequate definition of perception – one that necessitates the possibility of awareness. Nevertheless, they argue that perception without awareness does occur in the *ventral perceptual system* as: "the visual computations underlying unconscious perception seem to be identical to those underlying conscious perception: it's just that they don't make it into awareness."[29]

---

[29] Melvyn Goodale, David Milner, *Sight Unseen*, OUP, Oxford, 2004, p. 114.

Awareness, perception & experience

So, we can see conclude that there is a plethora of evidence which supports the idea that perception can exist without awareness.

Perception and Experience

Let us now consider the link between perception and experience. I have suggested that there are two different types of perception; let us first consider the perception of the senses. It is surely the case that this type of perception entails experience – when one's senses perceive the world this perceiving involves 'what-it-is-likeness'. This means that the perceptions which arise from the operations of one's senses are 'what-it-is-likeness' involving; that is to say, they are experience-involving.

What about the second type of perception? Well, as their name implies, the 'feeling perceptions' that pervade one's body are perceptions that are necessarily 'what-it-is-likeness' evolving; that is to say, they are necessarily experience-involving. So, as both types of perception involve experience this means that perception is an experience-involving activity.

Sleep and Dreaming

A full account of the relationship between awareness, perception and experience clearly needs to

Awareness, perception & experience

consider the phenomena of sleep and dreaming. We have already concluded that there are good reasons to believe that when one is awake that there are perceptions and experiences in one which one is unaware of. This being so, it is highly likely that there will also be perceptions and experiences in one which one is unaware of when one is asleep. Indeed, we have already considered such a case earlier in this essay.

One of the main questions before us is whether one can be both asleep and conscious/aware at the same time. According to David Papineau and John Searle one can be simultaneously asleep and conscious/aware:

Sometimes consciousness is explained as the difference between being awake and being asleep. But this is not quite right. Dreams are conscious too...Consciousness is what we lose when we fall into a dreamless sleep or undergo a total anaesthetic.[30]

"consciousness" refers to those states of sentience and awareness that typically begin when we awake from a dreamless sleep and continue until we go to sleep again, or fall into a coma or die or otherwise become "unconscious." Dreams are a form of

---

[30] David Papineau, *Introducing Consciousness*, Cambridge: Icon Books, 2005, pp. 4-5.

consciousness, though of course quite different from full waking states. Consciousness so defined switches off and on.[31]

So, according to Papineau and Searle, if one is asleep and dreaming one can contain the attribute of consciousness/awareness, but when one is asleep and not dreaming then one does not contain the attribute of consciousness/awareness. In other words, they believe that the attribute of awareness is discontinuous – it is an attribute which pops into and out of existence – and they draw the boundary of this 'popping' between states of wakefulness and

---

[31] John Searle, *The Mystery of Consciousness*, London: Granta Books, 1997, p. 5.

dreaming on the one hand, and states of dreamless sleep on the other.

This account of awareness clearly relies on one being aware of the dreams that one is having at the moment that one is having them. If one is not aware of the dreams as they are unfolding then one clearly does not possess the attribute of awareness when one is dreaming. If this is so, if one only becomes aware of the fact that one was dreaming when one *regains* awareness then clearly Papineau's and Searle's account will be inadequate.

Let us consider the phenomenon of 'lucid dreaming'. Stephen LaBerge explains the phenomenon as follows:

what happens when you become lucid? Essentially, you become explicitly aware of a particular important fact – that you are dreaming...if you were sleeping in a sleep lab with electrodes to record your eye-movements, you could mark the moment when you became lucid by, for example, looking to the left, right, left, and right in the dream. Then let's say you flew about your dream and then woke up a few minutes later and reported your dream. The polygraph would in fact show the eye-movement signal just when you reported.[32]

---

[32] Stephen LaBerge, in Susan Blackmore, *Conversations on Consciousness*, Oxford: OUP, 2005, p. 141.

What transition is occurring when one 'becomes lucid'? It is the transition from lacking the attribute of awareness to attaining the attribute of awareness. In other words, the phenomenon of 'lucid dreaming' means that Papineau and Searle's definitions need to be modified from "dreaming" to "lucid dreaming". Papineau and Searle are correct to assert that awareness is discontinuous but the boundary of the 'popping' actually appears to be between states of wakefulness and lucid dreaming on the one hand, and states of non-lucid dreaming and dreamless sleep on the other. Given that the vast majority of dreaming that exists in the world is 'non-lucid' it is accurate to say that dreaming is typically wholly devoid of awareness.

Awareness, perception & experience

What exactly is dreaming? I suggest that it is simply thought that is going on within one. So, one can be awake and aware of some of one's thoughts, or one can be asleep and not be aware of any of one's thoughts. If one contains the attribute of awareness then these thoughts can be a 'something' which one's awareness takes as an object; however, if one doesn't contain the attribute of awareness whilst dreaming then awareness cannot take the dream as its object whilst it is occurring. It is, of course, possible for a dream to be stored in memory and become a 'something' for awareness at a later time period. It should also be noted that when one is dreaming without awareness one still has the attribute of perception so things external to one can become incorporated into one's dreams.

All of our discussion so far has assumed that awareness is a discontinuous attribute – one that pops into and out of existence. The issue we have been concerned with is where exactly the 'popping' occurs. Does the 'popping' actually occur? Richard Unger considers and swiftly rejects Descartes view that there is no such 'popping':

> Descartes held, against common sense (and incorrectly) that there never were any periods of his sleep, in any night or day, when he

wasn't conscious; it *only appeared that way*.³³

On the account of perception, experience and awareness which has been favoured in this book Descartes would be correct to assert that there were never any periods where he wasn't 'thinking', 'perceiving' or 'experiencing'. However, as Unger, Searle, and Papineau claim, he would be wrong to assert that there are never any periods when he is devoid of 'awareness'.

---

[33] Peter Unger, *All the Power in the World*, Oxford: Oxford University Press, 2006, p. 46.

Conclusions about Awareness, Perception and Experience

I have outlined the dominant 'awareness as experience' paradigm which asserts that awareness and experience are one and the same state of the world. This view is rejected by both the 'higher-order monitoring' theorists and the panexperientialists who both believe that *experience can exist without awareness*.

Furthermore, I have suggested that *perception can exist without awareness*, and that perception is necessarily 'what-it-is-likeness'-involving / experience-involving. If this is so, then it obviously follows that *experience can exist without awareness*. This

Awareness, perception & experience

means that we have two different roads to the same conclusion that experience can exist without awareness.

I have also explored the links between these three phenomena and the states of sleep and dreaming. I have suggested that awareness is a discontinuous state, but that one can be continuously thinking, experiencing and perceiving. I have also suggested that the boundary between states of awareness and states lacking awareness is sometimes drawn at the wrong place – the correct division should be between lucid dreaming and waking states on the one hand, and non-lucid dreaming and non-dreaming sleep states on the other.

Other books by the author:

What is Creativity? : Originality, Art & Invention
(2011)

Conceptions of the Universe : How our conceptions of reality arise from the limitations of our perceptual apparatus (2011)

What is a Mind? (2011)

Can a Raindrop be in Pain : A consideration of the location & pervasiveness of pain and other states of feeling (2011)

Two Essays – What is 'What-it-is-likeness'? & How many human sense are there? (2011)

www.ingramcontent.com/pod-product-compliance
Lightning Source LLC
Chambersburg PA
CBHW071414040426
42444CB00009B/2248